The Everyday Gourmet

Making Great Meals in Less Time

Bill Briwa, C.E.C., C.H.E.

PUBLISHED BY:

THE GREAT COURSES
Corporate Headquarters
4840 Westfields Boulevard, Suite 500
Chantilly, Virginia 20151-2299
Phone: 1-800-832-2412
Fax: 703-378-3819
www.thegreatcourses.com

Bill Briwa, C.E.C., C.H.E.

Chef-Instructor
The Culinary Institute of America
at Greystone

A 1980 graduate of The Culinary Institute of America (CIA), Chef Bill Briwa has worked in the hospitality industry for more than 30 years and is a Certified Executive Chef and Certified Hospitality Educator. In addition to being the resident chef for The Hess Collection winery in California's Napa Valley, Chef Briwa owned and operated his own bistro and worked at Thomas Keller's award-winning restaurant The French Laundry. He was also the executive chef for The Wine Spectator Restaurant at the CIA at Greystone and served as an officer on the board of the St. Helena Farmers' Market. As culinary chair of the 2004 Napa Valley Wine Auction, Chef Briwa helped raise more than five million dollars for local charities. In addition to his work as a cook and chef, he has worked as both a baker and pastry chef. His writing on food and wine, olive oil, and cooking has been featured locally and in *Fine Cooking*, *Mise en Place*, and *Sunset*, as well as in the trade publications *Flavor & the Menu* and *Practical Winery & Vineyard Journal*.

As a Chef-Instructor at the CIA, Chef Briwa has developed curricula and has taught cooking, flavor dynamics, gastronomy, and food-and-wine pairing full time for the past 15 years. He has traveled to both teach and study cooking across the United States; in China, Mexico, South and Central America, and Europe; and around the Mediterranean. In addition, he is part of the Industry Services Group at the CIA and works closely with a broad range of corporate clients to help them realize their culinary goals.

Chef Briwa has been a speaker at many professional conferences, and he takes part in the Healthy Kitchens, Healthy Lives conference held twice each year at the CIA at Greystone. The conference is copresented by Harvard School of Public Health and the CIA. Chef Briwa has collaborated with Dr. Connie Guttersen, an instructor at the CIA and author of *The Sonoma Diet*, on numerous presentations on nutrition and cooking, including a course on the science of healthy cooking produced by The Great Courses. In 2003, Chef Briwa was a judge for the American Cheese Society, and in 2005, he presented on gastronomy at the annual conference of the International Association of Culinary Professionals. In 2005, 2006, and 2007, he presented at the International Foodservice Manufacturers Association's Chain Operators Exchange conference, and in 2008 and 2009, he spoke at the National Restaurant Association Show. Chef Briwa also presented at Beyond Extra Virgin IV, a conference on superpremium olive oil, in Verona, Italy.

Over the last 30 years of cooking and teaching, Chef Briwa has taken one short break from the stove to become a puppeteer. He lives in Yountville, California, with his wife and a border collie—both of whom think highly of his cooking.

Chef Briwa is the instructor for three other offerings in The Great Courses' *Everyday Gourmet* series: *Rediscovering the Lost Art of Cooking, Making Healthy Food Taste Great*, and *Essential Secrets of Spices in Cooking*. ∎

Table of Contents

Note to the Home Chef

The ingredient lists provided in this guidebook are for general reference only. Chef Briwa frequently substitutes or adds ingredients as he cooks and encourages you to do the same. The key to becoming a great chef is to learn about your ingredients and how they change in the process of cooking, to taste your food frequently as you develop a dish, and to be courageous enough to experiment in the kitchen.

The Everyday Gourmet:
Making Great Meals in Less Time

Whether or not you enjoy cooking, preparing food is a perpetual chore—a job to be done day in and day out. In recent years, many of us—myself included—have taken to eating out more often or have outsourced the task of cooking by taking advantage of prepared or convenience foods. Although these options work in a pinch, if you're like me, you quickly realize what you've given up by taking the easy way out: a defining and creative aspect of life. Food is associated with national identity and, in some cases, with social ritual; it's strongly connected to family and friendship. Cooking and eating together are intimate and sensual experiences. And preparing food is a chance to take part, literally, in the creative process—the process of creating human health and well-being. The many facets of food and cooking are what led me to become a chef, and I'm loath to relinquish control of such an important aspect of life to just any restaurant or corporation. But even I admit, regardless of how compelling the arguments are for cooking our own food, producing daily meals remains a chore.

In this six-lesson course, I will share some ideas and recipes to make feeding yourself, your friends, and your family easier and more satisfying. My perspective is that of a busy father and husband but also—and most importantly—a chef. Chefs work with food and take great joy and satisfaction in its preparation and service, but we also learn how to work efficiently and get high-quality results. We look into the refrigerator or the pantry and begin to assemble meals in our minds, and when we purchase food, we do so with a plan. This approach is essential to getting the job done.

This course will shift your perspective from that of a home cook to a professional. You'll learn strategies for streamlining your work in the kitchen and tips for giving your meal planning an organizational makeover. Of course, you'll also discover some simple dishes that are quick to prepare and versatile and have broad appeal. Throughout the course, we'll focus on three overarching goals that will make you a better cook:

- Developing an understanding of the workings of taste and flavor

- Mastering basic cooking techniques

- Searching out high-quality ingredients and learning what you can expect of them

The payoff for achieving these goals will come in the weeks and months of meal preparation that lie in your future. The results of your cooking will become more enjoyable to others, and your experience in the kitchen will become richer and more personally satisfying—not just a daily chore.

Best regards,

Bill Briwa, Chef-Instructor
The Culinary Institute of America

Into the Mind of a Chef
Lesson 1

Having home-cooked meals sounds like a great treat, especially if there's a cook in your family who is willing to do the work, but what if you're the cook and you also hold down a full-time job, are responsible for full-time care of children, or have other demands on your time? That's a different story altogether—a stressful story. This reality drives all of us to eat out more often than we should or even to downgrade "cooking" to warming up convenience food or snacking on foods we know we shouldn't eat. This course is all about strategies to help get you back on track to home-cooked meals. You'll learn recipes that can be quickly executed, methods to streamline your time in the kitchen, and tips to make the results of your cooking worth the effort. Our focus is not on five-ingredient dishes or meals that can be made in 10 minutes or less but on organizing your time in the kitchen and learning to think like a chef.

Tips from a Kitchen Professional

- The first step to achieving efficiency in the kitchen is to use a template to develop a weekly menu plan and make a shopping list from this plan before you head out to the grocery store.* Don't skip this step; if you do, chances are you'll have to return to the store later in the week to pick up missing ingredients, or you'll end up throwing food away.

Smart Step Saver

Always chop garlic and parsley together. That way, you're not flavoring your cutting board with garlic. You can also cover your cutting board with a piece of waxed paper or parchment paper so that you don't have to wash it repeatedly as you work.

- As you write out the week's menu, give thought to generating "planned-overs." Make double batches of soups, stews, or casseroles and freeze the extra for future meals. These stored

---

*See the Menu-Planning Template at the back of this guidebook. To download and print the template, go to www.thegreatcourses.com, log in to your customer account, select "Course Starter Materials," and then select *The Everyday Gourmet: Making Great Meals in Less Time.*

meals will be a lifesaver when you hit a busy week that doesn't allow time for cooking.

- Let ingredients that are in season and at their peak set the theme for your weekly menu. For example, summer tomatoes might inspire you to make pasta with fresh heirloom tomato sauce and basil one night and ceviche served with corn chips and salsa later in the week.

- Have on hand a selection of small containers to hold leftovers that might be repurposed for other meals.

Sautéing

For sautéing or other stovetop cooking, heat the pan before you add oil. Between the pan and the oil, the oil is more delicate and can withstand only a certain amount of heat.

- As soon as you come home from the supermarket to make a meal, even before you put away the groceries, turn the oven on; if you're making pasta, start a pot of water boiling on the stove.

- Always try to multitask in the kitchen. As meat is browning, unpack your groceries, periodically checking on the pans you've already got going. As one part of a dish is cooking, chop ingredients for the next step.

- Divide your time in the kitchen mentally into three parts. In the first third, you're working quickly—turning on the oven, putting pots of stock on to boil. During the second third, you're keeping up with the different tasks required of what you're cooking or doing prep work for future meals. For example, if you're washing lettuce for tonight's salad, you might as well wash tomorrow night's spinach at the same time. The last third is the payoff—your time to relax; focus on setting the table nicely and coasting home.

Tough v. Tender

As a general rule, the closer you get to the ground on a cow, the tougher the meat becomes. Think of the legs as an engine that moves the cow around, and the rest of the animal—the tender part—simply holds the engine together.

Osso Buco di Vitello

Ingredients

Yield: 6 portions

Osso buco:
- 1 medium onion, finely chopped
- ½ cup olive or vegetable oil
- 1 cup carrot, shredded
- 1 cup celery, finely diced
- 1 cup all-purpose flour
- Salt and freshly ground pepper to taste
- 6 pieces of veal shank, cut 2 inches thick and tied with twine
- 2 tsp tomato paste
- 1 cup dry white wine
- ½ cup carrot juice
- ½ cup orange juice
- 1 cup tomatoes, crushed
- 4 cups chicken stock
- Tarragon vinegar, to taste

Gremolata:
- 2 strips of lemon peel, yellow part only, finely chopped
- ¼ cup Italian parsley, finely chopped
- 1 clove garlic, finely chopped

Bouquet garni:
- 1 sprig fresh thyme
- 2 bay leaves
- 4 cloves garlic
- 3-inch celery stalk
- 1 sprig rosemary
- Orange zest

Of course, osso buco is not necessarily what you think of when you hear the words "quick cooking," but it's a dish that doesn't need your attention once it's started. You can have it cooking for an hour or two while you are busy with other things.

The first step in this recipe is to **truss** the meat, that is, to wrap the outside with a piece of string. The reason for doing this is that when it cooks, the meat becomes very tender, and without the string, it may fall apart. Next, season both sides of the veal with salt and pepper and dredge in flour. The flour captures all the juices as they seep out of the meat.

Heat a pan and add oil. When the oil begins to creep around the pan, add the meat and brown it for about 4 or 5 minutes.

Heat another pan to create an aromatic foundation for braising the meat. Again, after the pan is hot, add the oil, and when it heats up, add the diced onions. Typically, onions are cooked first in a recipe because they have a harsh, sulfurous quality, and cooking transforms that quality into sweetness. As the onions cook, they take on a different aroma and become translucent. That's an indication that the harsh quality has been eliminated. At that point, add the diced celery and carrots. You don't want to brown these vegetables; just cook them until they're tender. The onions, carrots, and celery are meant to lend their body and texture to the finished osso buco.

The next ingredient to add is tomato paste. Brown the tomato paste to take a bit of the harsh edge off it and make it richer. The French word for this step is *pincage*. Next, add tomatoes.

A tough cut of meat, such as this veal shank, has a good deal of collagen and connective tissue; thus, it needs to be cooked slowly in liquid after it has been browned. Slow cooking causes the collagen to melt into gelatin, which makes the meat tender and gives the dish a wonderful mouthfeel. Most cookbooks call for cooking osso buco in veal stock, but we'll use chicken stock, wine, carrot juice, and orange juice for a lighter, summery version of osso buco.

Note that at this point, you could transfer the meat and vegetables to a slow cooker and allow them to cook all day or overnight.

As the liquid comes to a boil, add the **bouquet garni**. You can make this by packing a piece of celery with a couple of cloves of garlic, some rosemary and

All about Rice

Rice comes in varying lengths compared to width. For example, in the United States, we seem to like long-grain rice, which tends to cook up loose and fluffy. In the eastern Mediterranean, medium-grain rice is used, which is about three times as long as it is wide. This rice cooks up less fluffy and a little sticky unless it is handled correctly. It must be rinsed to remove surface starch and then parched in hot oil so that each grain gets a proper coat of gelatinized starch on the outside and an oily overcoat that will keep each grain distinct from its neighbor.

Short-grain rice is about twice as long as it is wide and cooks up sticky. Many cultures capitalize on this sticky quality. Sushi, for example, holds together because of this stickiness, and this rice is usually just right for eating with chopsticks. Italian risotto gets its characteristic creamy texture and mouthfeel from this same short-grain rice.

thyme, and some orange zest. Wrap the celery in bay leaves and tie the package with a piece of string. If you like, you can tie the other end of the string onto the pot handle so that it's easy to find later. Transfer the browned veal to the pot with the liquid and vegetables and cook in a slow oven for about 2 hours.

The way to determine doneness with a piece of braised meat is to pierce the meat with a sharp knife; it should slide in and out easily. Sometimes, a sharp knife may go in quickly and easily, but when you pull it out, the meat hangs on a little bit. If that happens, cook the meat for a little longer. When it's done, remove the meat to a platter.

Everything that remains in the pan is the basis for your sauce. Remove the bouquet garni. Swirl a ladle around in the liquid to throw the fat to the outside of the pan, then skim it off. Next, put everything that remains in the pot into a blender. If you have a small blender, you may have to work in batches. When working with hot liquids, fill the blender no more than half full. Pulse to combine the vegetables into the sauce.

After it's blended, strain the sauce into a bowl. This sauce is wonderfully creamy and lighter in color than the dark, deep brown sauce you may have eaten with braised veal in the past. That lightness comes from the carrot and orange juice and chicken stock.

Have a taste of the sauce. If it's a bit too rich, add some acidity, such as a splash of tarragon vinegar. Because you used canned tomatoes, you probably don't need any salt. Make sure all the strings are removed from the meat before serving.

Saffron

Saffron is the stamen from a small crocus, and each flower has only three threads. Saffron threads lend food a wonderful color, aroma, and flavor. The way to get the most from saffron is to soak it in a little bit of hot liquid before using it in a dish. But make sure the liquid is not a fat. Oil will encapsulate the color and flavor of the saffron, preventing it from transferring to other ingredients.

When you cook a dish for a long time, there's always the possibility that the food may lose some of its vitality or freshness. To counter that, garnish the veal by sprinkling on **gremolata**, a condiment made from chopped parsley, garlic, and lemon zest.

This dish probably takes about 3 hours from start to finish, but the amount of active time needed at the stove is quite short.

The Risotto Kit

Learning the technique for making risotto can provide you with a lifetime of satisfying meals. The four parts of a "risotto kit" are as follows:

- *Sofrito*, or flavor base: The foundational flavors for risotto are usually derived from onion or shallots cooked in butter, celery, garlic, and perhaps a long-cooking, resinous herb, such as thyme, bay leaf, or rosemary. A small amount of chopped ham, sausage, bacon, or pancetta is also appropriate.

- Rice: Risotto is made with a specific type of rice. Arborio, carnaroli, or vialone naño are all appropriate rices for making risotto. There are some small differences in these rices, but the main one has to do with the balance between two different types of starch, amylose and amylopectin. The more amylopectin in the rice, the stickier and starchier it will be, while a higher amount of amylose will yield a slightly firmer rice that holds its shape more readily. Coincidentally, both medium- and long-grain rices have higher amounts of amylose than their short-grained kin.

- Broth: This is the liquid component in which the rice cooks. It can be vegetable stock, chicken broth, beef stock, clam juice, fish stock, wine, or even fruit juice. It should be hot (just at a simmer) to make the preparation go more quickly; you should have three to four times as much broth by volume as rice; and the broth should be tasty and properly seasoned.

- *Condimenti*: The *condimenti* or garniture often simply refers to the finishing ingredients, such as a knob of butter and a grating of cheese, but it may also include whipped cream; flavored compound butters; diced lobster or ham; tender and aromatic herbs that require little cooking; delicate vegetables, such as English peas or early-spring asparagus; sautéed wild mushrooms; roasted squash; or any number of other delicious add-ins, many of which might just be leftovers from a previous meal. If you think of risotto as a pasta—and that's really not too much of a stretch—then such additions as leftover Italian sausage, a little tomato sauce, and a handful of arugula begin to make delicious sense with a dusting of freshly grated Parmesan.

Risotto Milanese

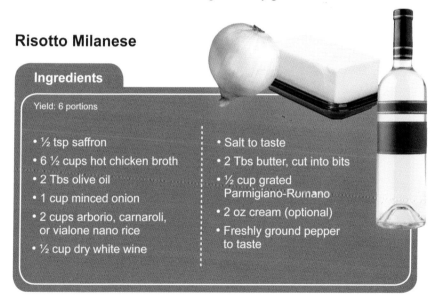

Ingredients

Yield: 6 portions

- ½ tsp saffron
- 6 ½ cups hot chicken broth
- 2 Tbs olive oil
- 1 cup minced onion
- 2 cups arborio, carnaroli, or vialone nano rice
- ½ cup dry white wine

- Salt to taste
- 2 Tbs butter, cut into bits
- ½ cup grated Parmigiano-Romano
- 2 oz cream (optional)
- Freshly ground pepper to taste

Unlike osso buco, which can simmer on its own for 2 hours or so, risotto requires your undivided attention—but only for about 20 minutes. Think of risotto not as a recipe but as a technique.

Begin by soaking the saffron in warm water. Then add it to hot, seasoned chicken stock. The reason the stock is heated is so that when it's added to the pan, it won't cool the rice down. For the *sofrito*—the flavor base—cook the minced onions in butter. Turn the heat up and add the arborio rice, coating it with the flavorful fat.

When you're making long-grain rice, you often add all the liquid at once, cover the pot, turn it down to a simmer, and walk away. But risotto is more demanding than that. It likes to have its starch brought out little by little. The way to accomplish that is to add the liquid incrementally. If you make the mistake of adding too much liquid all at once, the grains of rice give up their starch too quickly and lose their integrity.

The first addition is white wine. As you stir it in, you'll notice that the rice absorbs the wine quickly, but the wine doesn't completely cover the rice. Keep stirring as the mixture comes up to a simmer. By stirring, you're shearing the starch off the outside of the rice and mixing it with the liquid; you're also ensuring that the rice cooks evenly. Continue stirring for a minute or two until the liquid is almost completely absorbed.

The next addition is the saffron-flavored stock. You should have about three and a half to four times as much stock as rice by volume. Add the stock, a little at a time, and continue stirring. When you can see the bottom of the pan as you stir, add more stock. As you work, you'll see the creamy sauce that is the hallmark of great risotto begin to take form. The finished rice should be moist and should just barely hold its shape on a spoon without running or flowing. To test it, bite into a grain. If you can see any chalky core, the rice is not fully cooked; the same holds true for pasta.

From start to finish, risotto takes about 18 minutes. If you don't have that much time, you can practice "risotto interruptus": After you've added half the liquid, take the risotto out of the pan to cool. To finish the par-cooked risotto, warm it, introduce more hot stock, and start the stirring process again. The second round should take about 10 minutes. You might try this if you're making risotto and you want to save some for a subsequent meal.

When the risotto is done, stir in some butter, which will make the rice shine a bit and make it slightly looser, and cheese. Season it with salt and pepper. If you're serving this risotto by itself, you might add some peas to give it color. For our meal, spoon the rice onto a platter and transfer the osso buco on top, ladle on some of the sauce, and sprinkle with the gremolata and pepper.

Collecting Recipes

Your recipe collection may be a binder of ideas, a pile of papers, a box of index cards, a computer file, or a stack of dog-eared cookbooks with sticky notes marking the dishes you've tried and those you hope to try. Whatever its form, this collection represents your repertoire in the kitchen. And you can expand this repertoire by making a commitment to try new recipes and techniques. Trying just one new lunch and one new dinner a week expands your range by more than 100 recipes a year, and a new technique can offer any number of variations. To paraphrase an old saw: Give a man a chicken sandwich and you feed him for a day, but teach him to make a chicken sandwich, and he can feed himself and his family hundreds of variations on a theme or even open up a family chicken sandwich restaurant and make a fortune. Because food is such an important part of our lives, any small change that makes your cooking more interesting or the results better tasting is worth the time and effort it takes to incorporate.

As you add to your recipe collection—with recipes from friends or those you find in magazines or online—keep a running list of favorite dishes you like that aren't intimidating to make. These are the dishes you'll use most often to populate your weekly menus.

Important Terms

bouquet garni: A small package of herbs tied together and cooked with a dish but removed before serving.

condimenti: Refers to finishing ingredients of a dish, such as butter, grated cheese, and so on.

gremolata: A condiment made from chopped parsley, garlic, and lemon zest.

sofrito: Flavor base.

truss: To wrap meat with string to hold it together while it cooks.

Launching the Day

Lesson 2

Waking up in the morning, getting a cup of coffee, and getting out the door often seem like enough of a challenge in themselves without the added responsibility of cooking breakfast. But we all know that breakfast is the most important meal of the day, and many people feel shortchanged if they don't start the day with a good breakfast. In this lesson, you'll learn several ideas for breakfast foods that you can put together quickly, including muffins, cereal, and even fried rice; as you'll see, launching your day with a good breakfast doesn't have to mean adding too much time in the kitchen to your already busy routine.

Savory Breakfasts

You can make a delicious savory breakfast with some sliced ripe tomatoes, a handful of arugula, and "flavor bombs" that are almost always in your pantry or refrigerator: olives, pepperoncini, and cheese, such as Fontina, Manchego, or even simple cottage cheese. Dress the whole plate with a good-quality olive oil, salt, and pepper and serve with toast. Sweet breakfasts sometimes trigger people to continue eating sweets throughout the day, but a savory breakfast, such as this one, helps you avoid that trap.

Leavening

Whenever you see baking soda in a recipe, you should expect to add some acid, such as buttermilk. The baking soda needs to react with acid to give off carbon dioxide—that's the leavening that takes place.

Another great breakfast dish can be made with **tahini**—sesame paste; you may have some of this lingering in your refrigerator if you've ever made hummus or baba ghanoush. Spread a thin layer of tahini on a plate; on top, drizzle some honey mixed with pomegranate molasses. In Turkey, this dish is traditionally made with a product called **pekmez**, which is grape molasses. Pekmez may be difficult to find outside of Mediterranean grocery stores, but the combination of honey and pomegranate makes a delicious substitute. Serve the mixture with bread for dipping. The result tastes like peanut butter and jelly with a Turkish passport.

Breakfast Muffins

Ingredients

Yield: 12 muffins

- 1 ½ cups whole-wheat flour
- ½ cup white flour
- 1 Tbs baking powder
- ½ tsp baking soda
- ¾ tsp salt
- 3 eggs
- 1 cup buttermilk

- ¼ cup brown sugar
- 1 tsp vanilla
- 3 Tbs butter, melted
- 3 Tbs vegetable oil
- 1 ½ cups seasonal fruit, dried fruit, toasted nuts, or frozen corn kernels

If you like something sweet for breakfast, a muffin is a great option. Make these muffins with a mixture of whole wheat and white flour, or you can try flour made from **spelt**, an ancient kind of wheat. Mix together all the dry ingredients: flour, salt, baking soda, baking powder, and sugar. Make sure you break up any lumps of brown sugar.

For the wet ingredients, combine egg, buttermilk, melted butter, vegetable oil, and vanilla. At this point, think about what you might add to make this recipe more interesting, such as nuts, fruit, or granola. If you like the idea of a savory muffin, leave out a little bit of the sugar and add corn and green chiles. You might also add some cooked whole grains, such as barley, wheat berries, or brown rice. For these muffins, we'll add blueberries, nutmeg, and lemon zest. Other good combinations include walnuts and cherries, apples and carrots, blackberries and blueberries, or pistachios and apricots.

Combine the wet and dry ingredients, but be careful not to overmix the batter. Use a spatula instead of a whisk. The more you mix, the more gluten or protein will develop and the tougher the muffins will become. When the batter is almost completely mixed, add the blueberries.

Spoon the batter into a muffin pan lined with paper cups and bake for 10 to 15 minutes in a 400° oven. When you're making muffins, make a double batch and freeze some. You can take a muffin out of the freezer before you get dressed and eat it before you leave or take one with you on your way out the door to work.

Creating a Healthy Muffin

Here are a number of strategies you might consider when trying to create muffins with a healthier nutritional profile:

- Replace all or part of the white flour with whole-wheat pastry flour (which has a silky rather than a coarse feel). The flavor of your muffins will become nuttier and sweeter, and the texture will be slightly denser. Adding an extra ¼ to ½ teaspoon baking powder and an extra tablespoon of liquid per cup of whole-grain flour can compensate for these changes in whole-grain baking. You might also try replacing all-purpose flour with whole-grain spelt flour.

- Use protein powder to replace about ⅕ of the flour. In addition to a boost in protein, this substitution results in a slightly sweeter flavor and a firmer muffin.

- Rather than changing the type of flour you use in your favorite muffin recipe, consider simply adding cooked whole grains in much the same way you might add nuts or dried fruit. This strategy also works well with pancakes and waffles.

- Such additions as fresh, frozen, or dried fruit; nuts and seeds; and prepared cereals, such as granola, can boost the nutrition and appeal of a simple muffin recipe.

- For recipes that call for melted butter, you can replace the butter measure for measure with healthy oil, such as canola or olive oil. Healthy and flavorful nut oils can also be used, which add their own distinctive flavor. If replacing all of the butter seems too extreme, start by replacing just half; this alone represents a significant stride forward toward a healthier nutritional profile.

- The portion size of muffins is another important consideration. As appealing as oversized muffins might be, the calories can quickly mount to what you might expect to eat for an entire meal. Keep an eye out for smaller or "mini" muffin tins.

- Nonstick cooking sprays—without partially hydrogenated fats—make greasing muffin cups easy and efficient and can cut calories significantly. Even more effective is to use paper muffin liners and avoid the extra fat altogether.

- Remember that not all muffins need to be sweet. Savory whole-grain muffins, such as green chile–corn muffins, are a welcome treat both at breakfast or brunch and as an accompaniment to a bowl of soup or stew in the evening.

- Finally, keep in mind that flavor is a health issue: A healthy muffin that no one eats might just as well be considered a healthy bookend, paperweight, or doorstop.

Breakfast Cereal

Ingredients

Yield: 1 portion

- 1 cup whole-grain cereal mix (not instant)
- ½ cup dried fruits (prunes, figs, apricots, dates), roughly cut
- ½ cup nuts and seeds (walnuts, almonds, pumpkin seeds)

- ¼ cup flaxseed and sesame seeds
- ½ cup fresh fruits
- ½ cup plain yogurt

Many people reach for a box of cold cereal in the morning because it makes for an easy breakfast. They know that whole-grain cereal might be a better choice, but it takes too long make. With a little preparation, however, you can have a bowl of cooked whole-grain cereal in as little as 3 minutes.

Instead of oatmeal, try a cereal mix with multiple grains, such as rolled oats, barley, **farro** (an ancient form of wheat), or brown rice. A mix cooks in about 10 minutes, but if you soak it overnight, it will cook in about 3 minutes the next

morning. You should also take breakfast into account in your menu planning. If you're making barley for an evening meal, make extra to serve as breakfast the next morning. Or make extra cereal on the weekend and save it for weekday mornings. Put the cereal in a pan with a little bit of water, smooth it out, and in 2 minutes, you've got a good breakfast on the table.

Make a game of supplementing your cereal with nutritional add-ons. How many superfoods can you include? Start by rehydrating some dried fruit, such as raisins, cranberries, or apricots, right along with the grains as they cook. Next, add fresh fruit, such as raspberries, blueberries, strawberries, apples, or banana. For some protein, be sure to include chopped almonds, walnuts, or pecans. You can toast enough nuts ahead of time in the oven to last you for two or three weeks. On top, add a big dollop of yogurt and, if you like, a drizzle of honey. Finally, sprinkle on some toasted sesame seeds for a boost of nutty flavor, along with some flaxseed. Flax is a nutritional powerhouse, loaded with fiber and omega-3 oils. It's best to leave these seeds uncooked. If you don't like their flavor, grind up a little cinnamon along with the flaxseeds.

This breakfast includes 4 kinds of fresh fruit, 4 kinds of dried fruit, 3 kinds of nuts, 10 grains, and a sprinkle of sesame and flax, yet it took only a few minutes to put together and tastes far more satisfying than cold cereal from a box.

The Basics of Cooking Whole Grains

Cooked whole grains—served individually or in combination—can make a healthy, filling, and highly textured hot cereal for breakfast. Go to a natural food store and visit the bulk bins, where you'll find many varieties of grains. Buy small amounts of several kinds and experiment with cooking them.

If you can boil water, you can cook whole grains. In fact, boiling water is all you need to do. After that, the grains basically cook themselves. Your biggest challenge is to remember they are on the stove. Some grains need to cook longer than others, and different types absorb varying amounts of water (see chart). But with the exception of couscous and bulgur—which aren't really whole grains and only need to be soaked in hot water—the cooking method is essentially the same across the board:

- Begin by parching the grains. Toast them in a 350° oven until golden and aromatic, or heat 1 tablespoon olive oil in a saucepot over medium heat. Add the grains and cook until they start to pop and become aromatic.

- Add the prescribed amount of hot liquid and a pinch of salt. Bring to a boil, reduce the heat to the lowest possible setting, cover the pan tightly, and cook until all the water is absorbed. Don't peek or stir until the recommended simmering time has passed.

- Drain off any water that remains after the grains have become tender. Conversely, if the grains are crunchier than you'd like them or they're too dry, add a little water (up to ¼ cup) and let them cook 5 minutes longer.

- For a fluffy result, lightly comb through the cooked grains with a fork to let the steam escape. If you like the grains to be more like porridge, keep the pot covered after removing it from the heat and let it sit undisturbed for about 10 minutes before serving.

- Accompaniments are always welcome. Consider adding any of the following to cooked grains: fresh or dried fruit, toasted nuts, seeds, coconut, honey or pure maple syrup, milk or cream, or even a touch of butter.

All kinds of grains can be cooked in advance and reheated in a microwave or on the stovetop with a little extra liquid added. You can refrigerate cooked grains for several days and simply reheat them as needed in the morning.

Various types of cooked grains combine beautifully with each other. For optimal results, cook them separately per their individual requirements and then combine them only after they are done. (The only exception to this rule is millet and quinoa, which can be cooked together.) When mixing different grains, aim for a balance of flavor and texture; for example, combine intense, bitter, and chewy types with fluffier, sweeter ones.

Grain Cooking Chart

Grain	Grain-to-Water Ratio (Cups)		Simmering Time	Yield (Cups)
	Grain	Water		
Oat groats	1	2 ½	40–45 minutes	3 ½
Brown rice, including basmati	1	2 ½	35–45 minutes	3 ½
Wild rice	1	2 ½	75 minutes or until tender	4
Pearl barley	1	3	90 minutes or until tender	4
Quinoa	1	1 ½	20 minutes or until tender	3
Millet	1	1 ½	25–30 minutes	3
Fluffy quinoa and millet	1 each	3	30–35 minutes; transfer to a pan, spread out, and separate with a fork to allow steam to escape	6
Buckwheat groats/kasha	1	1 ½	10 minutes	3 ½
Cracked wheat	1	2	10 minutes	3 ½
Amaranth	1	1 ¾	25 minutes	2
Wheat berries	1	3	2–2 ½ hours for hard (red) wheat, shorter time for soft (white) wheat	3
Spelt	1	1 ½	50–60 minutes	2
Kamut	1	2 ½	35–45 minutes	3 ½
Rye berries	1	2 ½	35–45 minutes	3 ½
Bulgur, medium	1	2 ½	No cooking involved; soak grain in boiling water for 30–40 minutes	3 ½

Egg Fried Rice

Ingredients

Yield: 4 portions

- 2 large eggs
- ½ tsp salt
- 2 Tbs peanut or canola oil
- ½ cup mushrooms, sliced
- 2 large scallions, finely chopped
- ¼ cup carrots, cut to ¼-inch dice
- 2 oz deli ham, cut to ¼-inch dice (optional)

- 1 cup asparagus, cut to 1 inch and blanched
- 3 ½ cups long- or medium-grain cold cooked rice (white/brown or combination)
- 2 tsp soy sauce
- ½ tsp sesame oil
- Cilantro for garnish

Fried rice might seem like a surprising choice for breakfast, but if you think about it, this dish contains many foods you might already eat in the morning: ham, eggs, grains, and leftover vegetables. Because stir-frying is a fast technique, this dish also helps you get out the door quickly.

The first step is to make a thin omelet. Heat a pan (preferably nonstick) and crack two eggs into it. Because fried rice is an Asian dish, use soy sauce as a seasoning rather than salt and pepper. As the eggs get close to being done, spread them out in a thin layer. When they're done, slide them onto your cutting board and allow them to cool before slicing into pieces.

Next, begin heating a wok or sauté pan. As the pan is heating, slice up some trumpet mushrooms. Discard the stems, but cut the mushrooms into pieces that are easily distinguishable. Cut some carrots on a long bias. To these ingredients, add chopped scallions, diced ham, and blanched asparagus. (Blanching allows vegetables to hold onto their color better than if they are sautéed raw.)

When the wok or pan is hot, add some oil. As soon as it begins to smoke, put in the mushrooms and carrots, which take the longest to cook. A wok cooks efficiently because it's designed to constantly move the food back to the hottest part of the pan. If you're stir-frying foods that are tough or resist getting tender, you can always splash in a little water to steam them.

Next, add the ham and green onions. What you're doing here is creating a flavorful fat in which to cook the rice. It's best to use rice for this dish that has

been cooked ahead of time and refrigerated. And you don't need to use rice only; you can toss in other grains, such as wheat or barley. Multiple grains give the dish visual texture and a nutty flavor. As you're stir-frying the grains, break up any lumps, and if they start to stick, add a little more oil. Press the grains down against the pan to sear them.

When the rice is hot and the mushrooms and carrots are cooked, add the egg and asparagus, both of which have already been cooked and just need to heat up. Season the dish with pepper and more soy sauce, adding the soy to the hot pan so that it begins to reduce. It shouldn't color the dish too much but just flavor it. In many Chinese dishes, sesame oil is added at the end. This oil is very aromatic, but if it's added too early, the aroma is lost. Drizzle sesame oil on the fried rice, sprinkle on some cilantro, and serve. If you have any leftovers, you can take this fried rice to work the next day and heat it in a microwave.

Important Terms

farro: An ancient form of wheat.

pekmez: Grape molasses used in Turkey.

spelt: An ancient form of wheat.

tahini: Sesame paste; used to make hummus or baba ghanoush.

One Fresh Thing

Lesson 3

Raiding the pantry for convenience food may seem like heresy in a cooking course, but not even professional chefs cook everything from scratch. For many meals, you can add fresh ingredients to leftovers or prepared foods to enhance their flavor and make them seem like something new for your friends and family. In this lesson, we'll see how just a fresh tomato, a squeeze of lemon, or a couple of sausage links can help you put dinner on the table in as little as 20 minutes after a full day at work. We'll also talk about planning ahead as you cook so that you can take advantage of leftovers for multiple quick meals.

Toasted Bread with Tomato, Catalan Style

Ingredients

Yield: 4 portions

- 8 large, thin slices French-style bread
- 2 cloves garlic, peeled and cut lengthwise
- 2 large, very ripe tomatoes, cut crosswise
- 2 Tbs olive oil
- 1 tsp salt
- ¼ tsp ground black pepper

When your objective is to prepare a quick meal, think in terms of simplicity and what you have on hand, but add fresh ingredients to make something different. For instance, for toasted bread with tomato, you can start with stale bread leftover from a previous dinner. Toast the bread and rub a peeled garlic clove across the surface. Once the bread is flavored with garlic, cut a fresh, ripe tomato in half, squeeze out some of the seeds, and rub the tomato over the toast, too. Think of the toast as a grater; what should be left behind is a little bit of tomato skin and not much more.

Next, drizzle on extra-virgin olive oil and season with salt and pepper. Enjoy the bread with a fried egg, a bowl of soup, or a salad.

Using fresh ingredients in unique ways is one strategy for putting together quick and pleasing meals.

Planning Ahead

One item you almost always have in your pantry that can be used to make a quick meal is beans. Of course, you can't make beans from scratch in a hurry, but if you plan ahead, you can make a pot of beans on a Sunday afternoon while you're watching a game on TV and put them aside for meals later in the week. You can even put them in the freezer for two or three months.

First, shake the beans out on a tray and sort through them to remove any rocks or clumps of dirt. Next, cover them with water and soak overnight. Use about three times as much water as beans. Notice that the soaked beans are almost twice the size of the dry ones. Beans take some time to rehydrate, but you certainly don't have to monitor the process while they soak.

Canned beans are also convenient to have in your pantry, but they're often loaded with salt. If you make the beans yourself, you can control the salt content and add other flavorings. Here, you can add a couple of bay leaves, a sprig of rosemary, a sprig of thyme, some pepper flakes, even some dried mushrooms, garlic, or onion. Keep

Cooling Food Safely

If you cook extra beans to save for another meal, you need to cool them from the temperature at which they cooked to 70° in 2 hours; then, from 70°, you need to cool them to refrigerator temperatures (30°–38°) in the following 2 hours. To do this, transfer the beans to a shallow container that conducts heat well, such as a glass pie plate. Don't use a deep plastic container because the plastic is an insulator, not a conductor of heat. Once the beans are cold, then you can keep them in a plastic container or even a gallon-size plastic bag; store them in the refrigerator for a week or in the freezer for a month.

in mind, however, that if you add too many distinctive ingredients, the beans become less versatile. If you can make them taste good but also give them broad appeal, then you can use them in an Italian dish, a Mexican dish, or an American dish.

Once the beans come to a boil, skim off any accumulated foam and turn the heat down to a gentle simmer. Cook the beans for about 1 hour and 15 or 30 minutes. When they're done, the beans should hold their shape. If they start to fall apart, it's probably because you're cooking them too aggressively. They are boiling too hard and rubbing against one another. To test the beans for doneness, squeeze one between your fingers. You shouldn't see any chalky white in the middle; the bean should be velvety all the way through.

If you have cooked the beans for an hour and half and they're still not done, it may be that the beans are old and need to cook longer. Another problem may be that there is too much acidity in the beans. To remedy this, sprinkle just a pinch (¼ tsp) of baking soda into the water. Don't add too much baking soda, or the beans will taste soapy. When you sprinkle in the baking soda, you'll see it bubble up; that's a sign of acidity, which the baking soda will neutralize. You can then continue cooking the beans, and they'll become tender quickly.

To use the beans for other dishes, remove the herbs and vegetables you added. If you plan to use canned beans for a dish, drain them, but save the liquid. That's the best vegetable stock you can imagine. Like veal or chicken stock, it has body and viscosity, but it's all vegetables.

Salad of White Beans, Sausages, and Arugula with Basil Vinaigrette

Ingredients

Yield: 6 portions

Basil vinaigrette:
- 1 shallot, minced
- 1 lemon, juiced
- Zest of ½ lemon
- 1 Tbs Dijon mustard
- ⅓ cup extra-virgin olive oil
- Salt and pepper to taste
- Sugar to taste

Salad:
- 1 can white beans (15 oz) or fresh cannellini or great northern beans
- 1 large green bell pepper, cored, seeded, and diced
- 1 large tomato, seeded and diced
- 1 medium red onion, diced
- 1–2 tsp prepared pesto
- 2 links (about 7 oz each) cooked chicken or other favorite sausage
- 12 cups arugula, torn

One quick meal you can make with beans is salad. Begin by making the dressing, and always make more than you need. Start with a tablespoon or so of mustard, which acts as an **emulsifier**, helping the lemon juice and oil to mix. Add some shallots and salt and pepper, then squeeze in some lemon juice as your "one fresh thing." Whisk these ingredients and continue whisking as you add oil. Again, if you plan to make extra dressing and use it for additional meals, keep it as neutral and versatile as possible. Don't add basil, tarragon, Parmesan cheese, or anchovies. The proportions for vinaigrette are usually three parts oil to one part acid. Because this salad includes sausage, you might make the dressing a bit more tart to counter that richness. Set some dressing aside for a future meal.

Cook some sausage that you might have on hand, such as Italian sausage, breakfast sausage, or chorizo—check your refrigerator to see what you need to use up. Slice the sausage and add it to a serving of beans. Toss some greens with diced red onion, green pepper, tomato, the vinaigrette, and some pesto—one of the "flavor bombs" from your pantry. Season with salt and pepper and top with the bean and sausage mixture.

If you have beans you've cooked earlier or you use canned beans and have some dressing in the refrigerator, you could put this meal together in just the time it takes to cook two sausages. If you have some salad left over, you can take it to work the next day for lunch.

Baked Minestrone

Ingredients

Yield: 6 portions

- ½ lb cannellini beans, soaked overnight in abundant water (1:3 ratio of beans to water)
- ⅓ cup olive oil
- 2 yellow onions, sliced into thin rings
- 2 garlic cloves, minced
- 1 lb tomatoes, cut to ½-inch dice
- ½ lb green beans, cut into ¾-inch pieces
- 2–3 medium zucchini, sliced
- 1 bunch/head chard or escarole, ribbed and cut in ribbons
- ¼ cup flat-leaf parsley, minced
- 4 Tbs basil, chiffonade
- Salt and pepper to taste
- ¼ cup extra-virgin olive oil
- Freshly grated Parmesan cheese

Another dish you can make from the same batch of beans (or from canned beans in your pantry) is baked minestrone. Begin by sweating some onions in a pot until they're translucent; once the onions are cooking, add some garlic. Next, add tomatoes, either canned or fresh. You want to put something on the bottom of the pan that has a lot of moisture in it. To the tomatoes, add some green beans, sliced zucchini, white beans, and finally, greens, such as kale, escarole, chard, or spinach. Slice the greens into ribbons and put the ribbons on top. The liquid that goes into this soup includes the liquid from the drained beans and some chicken broth, either homemade and frozen ahead of time or

bought at the store and stored in your pantry. As an interesting flavor bomb, you can also toss in the rind that's left after you've grated a wedge of Parmesan cheese. There's a tremendous amount of flavor in the rind, and it will soften but not melt in the soup.

Flavor Bombs

Olives
Pepperoncini
Cheese
Pesto sauce
Sun-dried tomatoes
Capers
Dijon mustard
Soy sauce
Dried or canned chiles
Good-quality olive oil

Bring the soup to a boil, then cover it and turn it down to a simmer, or put the pot in a 350° oven. As the soup cooks, the starch from the beans will give the broth a great deal of body; the greens will wilt; and the tomatoes will begin to fall apart.

Taste the soup before adding salt, particularly if you used canned beans or purchased stock. For additional seasonings, add chopped parsley and basil or a bit of pesto from a jar. To prevent the basil from turning black, roll the leaves into a cigar and chop finely (**chiffonade**). Finish with some ground black pepper and grated Parmesan cheese.

This soup comes together in about 20 minutes. Serve it with the Catalan toast we made earlier and, of course, a glass of red wine.

Fritatta with Cauliflower and Sautéed Mushrooms

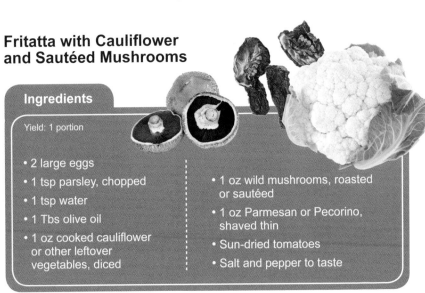

Ingredients

Yield: 1 portion

- 2 large eggs
- 1 tsp parsley, chopped
- 1 tsp water
- 1 Tbs olive oil
- 1 oz cooked cauliflower or other leftover vegetables, diced
- 1 oz wild mushrooms, roasted or sautéed
- 1 oz Parmesan or Pecorino, shaved thin
- Sun-dried tomatoes
- Salt and pepper to taste

A **frittata** can become your go-to meal any time of the day: breakfast, lunch, or dinner. This dish is quite easy, and you almost always have the ingredients to make it: eggs and leftovers.

Begin with the leftovers you have on hand, such as sautéed mushrooms, cooked cauliflower, and risotto. From your pantry or refrigerator, you might add some sun-dried tomatoes. Use just enough eggs to bind these ingredients together and stir. You could also add some herbs or green onions, but if you plan to serve the frittata with a salad, these additions aren't necessary. Season with salt and pepper, but keep in mind that the leftovers are seasoned already, so you want to add only enough salt and pepper to season the eggs.

Heat a nonstick pan and add some olive oil. Pour in the frittata mixture, making sure that all the ingredients are coated with egg. Turn the heat down if necessary so that the eggs cook gently—not too aggressively. As it's cooking, the frittata should move freely in the pan.

When the egg is almost completely set, use the pan lid to flip the frittata over. If you're nervous, you may want to do this step over the sink. Slide the frittata back into the pan and turn the heat down a little more. You might even turn the burner off because there is plenty of residual heat to finish cooking the dish. Shape the frittata a bit with a spatula while some of the egg remains uncooked. Top it off with some grated cheese. When it's done, the center should still be just a little moist.

While the frittata is cooking, make a small salad of arugula and radicchio, dressed with the vinaigrette we made earlier. Remember, you can store this vinaigrette in a jar in the refrigerator and just give it a good shake when you're ready to use it.

Slide the frittata onto a plate and serve immediately with some of the salad on top, seasoned with pepper. Or you can make a sandwich with the salad and frittata to take to work with you for lunch.

Important Terms

chiffonade: Finely sliced or shredded herbs or vegetables; often used as a garnish.

emulsifier: In cooking, an ingredient that helps hold otherwise immiscible liquids, such as oil and water, together in a mixture.

frittata: A dish that's similar to an omelet but unfolded. A good vehicle for using up leftover vegetables and preparing a quick meal.

Evolution of a Quick Dish

Lesson 4

Chowder may be the quintessential quick meal, originally cobbled together by fishermen at the end of a hard day at sea. In this lesson, we'll trace the evolution of chowder from this beginning and see the many variations that have emerged over the years. Today, chowder still makes a cozy meal for a cold evening, and as we'll see, it can also be dressed up to serve as a sauce for fish or chicken when you have guests. By the end of this lesson, you'll be an expert on chowder, ready to carry on the tradition of adapting it into the future.

The Story of Chowder

The original chowder was made onboard fishing boats from a meager pantry: the fish that had been caught during the day, fresh water, salted pork, and ship's biscuits, or hardtack. The fishermen would render the pork for its fat, layer in hardtack and fish steaks, and add fresh water and some salt water for seasoning. The mixture would then be simmered until it became a gruel.

Back on shore, this dish could take on a little more sophistication. The fish could be filleted and cut into cubes, and the cook could make a fish stock. The hardtack, which was often moldy or infested with insects—or both—could be replaced with potatoes to thicken the soup. Celery, onions, and a little bit of cream and butter could be added. At some point, clams were added, and clam chowder was born.

With the advent of the automobile, people who lived in cities could travel to the shore for rest and recreation. There, they ate all kinds of seafood—lobster, swordfish, and chowder—and when they went back home, they asked for the dishes by name. Chowder became so popular that Italian restaurateurs who had been making what they called "clam soup" for years rechristened the dish Manhattan chowder.

Eventually, the idea of chowder made its way west; the clams were dropped, because they weren't available, and cooks made farmstead chowder from corn or chicken. In the Midwest today, you can find chowder made with ground beef and cheese—cheeseburger chowder—and in the Southwest, it's made with smoked chicken and green chiles. When you reach the West Coast, clam chowder reappears on the wharves of San Francisco, served inside a hollowed-out loaf of sourdough bread.

New England Clam Chowder

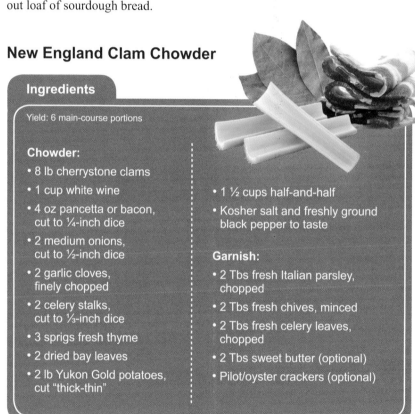

Ingredients

Yield: 6 main-course portions

Chowder:
- 8 lb cherrystone clams
- 1 cup white wine
- 4 oz pancetta or bacon, cut to ¼-inch dice
- 2 medium onions, cut to ½-inch dice
- 2 garlic cloves, finely chopped
- 2 celery stalks, cut to ⅓-inch dice
- 3 sprigs fresh thyme
- 2 dried bay leaves
- 2 lb Yukon Gold potatoes, cut "thick-thin"

- 1 ½ cups half-and-half
- Kosher salt and freshly ground black pepper to taste

Garnish:
- 2 Tbs fresh Italian parsley, chopped
- 2 Tbs fresh chives, minced
- 2 Tbs fresh celery leaves, chopped
- 2 Tbs sweet butter (optional)
- Pilot/oyster crackers (optional)

Let's begin by making New England clam chowder. You can use cherrystone clams or littlenecks for this dish. Rinse the clams well to remove any sand or mud. If you find an open clam, press it once or twice; if it closes up, it's still alive. If it doesn't, the clam is dead, and you should discard it. Steam the rest of the clams open in white wine.

In another pot, render some bacon. The idea here is to get the fat out of the bacon to be used in cooking the dish. If the bacon starts to brown before the fat has rendered out, add a little bit of water to the pot. Add the onions and celery to the bacon fat.

When the clams are all open, lift them out of the liquid and set aside to cool. Lifting the clams out of the pot allows you to leave behind any remaining grit or sand. Pour the clam broth carefully into the soup pot; again, you're likely to see some sand on the bottom of the pot, and you don't want to add that to your soup.

To the chowder flavor base, add all-purpose potatoes, such as Yukon Gold or Kennebec. Don't use russet potatoes because they tend to fall apart as they simmer, and don't use boiling potatoes because they don't fall apart at all and don't lend any body to the broth. Cut the potatoes into shapes almost like small ax heads, with a thick part and a thin part. As the potatoes cook, the thin part will break down and thicken the broth, while the thick part remains behind. Add some thyme, a couple of bay leaves, and some garlic if you like, and simmer the chowder until the potatoes are tender. While the broth is simmering, remove the clams from the shells and cut them into bite-sized pieces.

When the chowder is just about done, add the cream or milk and the clams and season the soup, tasting before you add any salt. If you think it needs more body, crush some of the potatoes against the side of the pot for thickening. If you have time, let the chowder stand for an hour on the stove to allow the flavors to mingle before you serve it. For serving, add a pat of butter to enrich the broth and sprinkle on some coarsely chopped parsley and chives. Place oyster crackers on the side—a nod to the original chowder made with hardtack.

A Modern-Day Variation

The story of chowder doesn't end in the United States. If you travel to Spain, you'll discover that clams are often combined with **chorizo**. For this variation, we'll first make potato-crusted cod and serve it with clam-chorizo chowder.

The first step is to skin the fish, such as a piece of lingcod. Start at the tail end and cut through the meat but not through the skin. You want to leave about an inch of skin so that you've got a handle. Then, glide your knife between the skin and the meat, pulling back on the skin from the tail end. Don't angle the knife too far down toward the skin or you'll cut through it; nor should you angle the knife too far upward or you'll cut into the meat. Try to glide the knife parallel to the cutting board. As the knife pushes forward, move the skin back.

Lingcod has pin bones, which can be removed from some types of fish with tweezers. But because the pin bones in lingcod don't pull out cleanly, you need to cut them out. Feel where each bone is with your fingers and cut down next to it on either side. Remove the bones and discard with the skin. You should be left with a piece of fish that is about 4 ounces.

As you're skinning and boning the fish, have some chunks of chorizo and garlic sautéing in a pan and keep the chowder that we made earlier hot.

The next step is to bread the fish with instant mashed potato flakes. Salt and pepper the fish on both sides. Dip it into flour and pat off the excess. Then, dip it into egg and allow the excess to drip off. Finally, coat it with the potato flakes. Move the chorizo to the side of the pan and allow the fish to cook in its flavorful fat. Once the fish is golden on one side, flip it over. Fish usually cooks in about 8 minutes per inch of thickness. A piece of fish that's ¾ of an inch thick will take about 6 minutes. You want the fish to be just opaque but still moist in the center.

In Spain, this dish is often served with a garlic mayonnaise—**aioli**. You can make this with commercial mayonnaise, thinned out with some broth from the soup. The idea here is to get a sensuous, pourable consistency. Add a little bit of garlic and lemon zest.

Add the chorizo to the chowder and serve it almost like a sauce or a bed for the fish. Garnish the plate with a couple of clams that you've left in their shells, a sprinkle of parsley, and a dollop of aioli on the fish. The same soup you had for dinner last night has now become a dish suitable for guests.

Farmhouse Corn Chowder

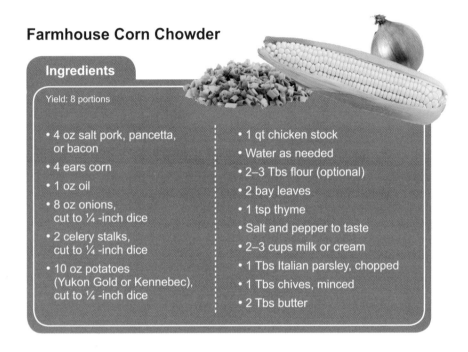

Ingredients

Yield: 8 portions

- 4 oz salt pork, pancetta, or bacon
- 4 ears corn
- 1 oz oil
- 8 oz onions, cut to ¼ -inch dice
- 2 celery stalks, cut to ¼ -inch dice
- 10 oz potatoes (Yukon Gold or Kennebec), cut to ¼ -inch dice

- 1 qt chicken stock
- Water as needed
- 2–3 Tbs flour (optional)
- 2 bay leaves
- 1 tsp thyme
- Salt and pepper to taste
- 2–3 cups milk or cream
- 1 Tbs Italian parsley, chopped
- 1 Tbs chives, minced
- 2 Tbs butter

As we saw, the story of chowder doesn't end when you leave the ocean behind. For this farmhouse chowder, the ingredients are different, but the technique remains the same.

Again, render bacon in a pot, remove the bacon and set aside, and then add onions, celery, a sprig of thyme, and a couple of bay leaves. If you like a thicker, more robust soup, you could add some flour and make a **roux**. This strategy will allow you to use a low-fat dairy product, such as half-and-half, in place of cream or even milk, which tends to break. Mix the flour with the flavorful fat in the pot.

Instead of clam liquor for the soup, use chicken broth. As it comes to a boil, the flour will thicken. Break up any lumps and add more broth. With each

progressive addition of liquid, the flour will become looser. Don't evaluate consistency until the mixture comes to a boil. Every starch thickens at a different temperature, but all of them are completely thickened at a boil.

After you stir in the rest of the chicken stock, add the potatoes. Again, it's best if these are cut a little unevenly so that the smaller pieces give body to the soup and the thicker pieces remain.

The next ingredient is corn, which provides starch that will also thicken the soup. White corn is usually more tender and sweeter than yellow, but yellow corn offers a full, rich flavor. To cut corn off the cob, place a small bowl upside down inside a larger bowl. Rest the cob on the smaller bowl as you cut off the kernels with a knife. Scrape the back of your knife over the cob to get all the corn milk off the cob. You can even put the whole cob into your soup to get more flavor and remove it before serving. Bring the soup to a boil, then simmer until the potatoes and corn are cooked. Reduce the heat and enrich with cream or milk.

If you decide that the soup is still not thick enough, stir some flour and water together in a small bowl to create a slurry. This slurry has all of the starch granules separated in a liquid matrix. Use this to make small adjustments to the thickness of the soup. Once the soup is at a boil, stir in a small amount of slurry,

then let the liquid come back to a boil before you reevaluate the consistency. Adding starch in this way keeps the soup more robust and helps prevent the milk or half-and-half from breaking.

Break up the bacon and add it back to the soup for textural interest. Add some salt, cracked pepper, and chives and serve the soup in rustic bowls. Because this chowder is thickened with flour, it holds up well from one day to the next. On the second day, you can even treat it as more of a sauce than a soup. Serve it on an **airline chicken breast**, alongside green beans and sautéed mushrooms.

Important Terms

aioli: Mayonnaise flavored with garlic.

airline chicken breast: A boneless chicken breast with part of the wing still attached.

chorizo: Spicy Spanish sausage.

roux: A combination of flour and fat, cooked together and used to thicken soups or sauces.

Chowder Variations

New England Clam Chowder,
with salt pork, onions,
clams, and potatoes

Midwest Corn Chowder,
with salt pork, corn,
onions, and potatoes

Southern Ham Chowder,
with ham, carrots, and potatoes

Spanish Clam-Chorizo Chowder,
with chorizo, garlic, and clams

Cheeseburger Chowder,
with ground beef, onion,
carrots, and cheddar cheese

Mexican Clam Chowder,
with white wine, clams,
avocados, and cilantro

French Fish Chowder,
with codfish and halibut,
white wine, and tomatoes

What Makes a Meal?

Lesson 5

A fter a long day at work, many people aren't interested in a four-course dinner, but they don't want convenience food either. What they want is something quick and satisfying that "feels" like a meal but isn't too heavy and doesn't involve extensive preparation. The key here is to change your thinking about what you consider a meal. For example, a simple cheese course accompanied by some seedless grapes, brushed with sherry vinegar and roasted in the oven, makes a filling dinner and doesn't seem thrown together. Instead of grapes, you could serve some ripe figs or strawberries from the farmers' market, along with some toasted almonds and cheese. In this lesson, we'll make a number of easy dishes that will transform your concept of "dinner."

Upscale Grilled-Cheese Sandwich à la Zuni Café

Ingredients

Yield: 4 portions

- 8 slices sourdough bread, sliced ¼-inch thick
- 3 Tbs whole-grain mustard

- ½ lb Fontina cheese, sliced
- 2 oz butter, softened
- 1 bunch fresh sage leaves

Almost everyone likes grilled cheese sandwiches, and you can make them just special enough to make a meal. Put a little mustard on both sides of the bread, followed by some Fontina—enough so that it will ooze out when heated. Spread some butter on the outside of the bread and press a couple of sage leaves into the butter. As the sandwich cooks, the sage will begin to brown and get crispy, perfuming the whole sandwich. Use the same technique for both sides of the sandwich and allow it to cook slowly—for about 10 minutes. You want the bread to brown and the cheese inside to soften and begin to melt.

Something Warm Makes a Meal

Sometimes, the addition of just one warm component can turn a snack into a meal. Consider, for example, the elements for Romeo and Juliet, a snack or appetizer made with Manchego cheese from Spain and membrillo, or quince

paste. To this, we'll add some sautéed Padrón peppers, also from Spain, and warmed Marcona almonds.

Padrón peppers are sometimes called Russian roulette peppers because in every batch of 8 or 10 peppers, there's one that's very hot. Typically, the larger peppers are the ones that tend to be hot, but there's no guarantee. Sauté the peppers in hot olive oil to blister the outside and just start to cook the flesh. Season with salt, and toward the end of the sauté time, add some Marcona almonds, just to warm them. Serve with Manchego cheese and membrillo for a meal that offers something warm, something savory, and something sweet.

Pappa al Pomodoro (Italian Tomato Soup)

Ingredients

Yield: 6 portions

- 3 lb ripe, red tomatoes, washed, cored, and roughly chopped
- 12 sprigs Italian parsley, chopped
- 1 red chile, minced
- 2 cloves garlic, minced

- 1 qt chicken stock
- 6 slices day-old rustic bread
- 4 oz Parmesan cheese, finely grated
- 1 cup extra-virgin olive oil
- Salt and pepper to taste

When ripe tomatoes are plentiful, there's no better meal than tomato soup. This Italian version, **pappa al pomodoro**, requires only a few basic ingredients.

Core the tomatoes and chop them into large chunks. Don't even bother removing the seeds or skin. Add the chopped tomatoes to a pot with chicken stock and a couple of smashed garlic cloves. To this mixture, add a Calabrian red chile. If you like your food spicy, cut up the whole chile; if you want to tone the heat down a bit, remove the seeds and ribs, which together hold about 80 percent of the heat of a pepper. Avoid touching your eyes or face when you're working with peppers and make sure to wash your hands with soap afterward to eliminate all traces of capsaicin—the chemical substance that makes chiles hot. Finally, toss in some chopped parsley, reserving a little for garnish. Bring this soup to a boil, then turn it down to a simmer for about 20 or 25 minutes.

After the simmering time, the tomatoes, garlic, and pepper will be soft. The next step is to coarsely puree those ingredients, preferably using a food mill. Return the puree to the broth. Don't worry if it looks a little thin at this point because you will add croutons to the finished soup.

Take a taste and season the soup. You may be surprised at how much salt it needs; the compounds in tomatoes result in a flavor described as **umami**, that is, a savory taste that demands a good deal of seasoning. Again, don't worry if the soup seems a little lean because you will add olive oil, and don't worry if it tastes less than complex because you will also add Parmesan cheese.

To a bowl, add some croutons made from a stale loaf of country bread. You can make these croutons ahead of time and keep them in the freezer. Cut the crust off leftover bread, tear it into small pieces, spread the pieces out on a baking sheet, drizzle with some olive oil, and bake for a few minutes.

To the croutons, add some parsley and a generous dollop of good-quality, "punchy" olive oil. Ladle the soup on top and give it a minute or so to soften the bread. Top with grated cheese and pepper. This simple soup makes a quick and satisfying dinner and will keep nicely in the refrigerator for a week.

Cauliflower Steak with Pancetta and Capers

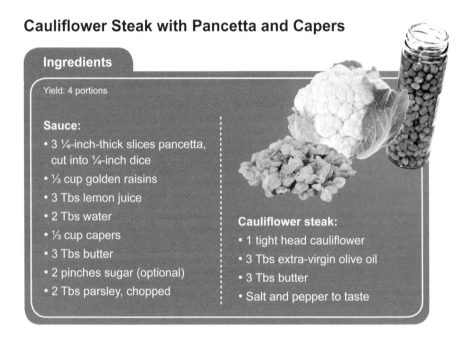

Ingredients

Yield: 4 portions

Sauce:
- 3 ¼-inch-thick slices pancetta, cut into ¼-inch dice
- ⅓ cup golden raisins
- 3 Tbs lemon juice
- 2 Tbs water
- ⅓ cup capers
- 3 Tbs butter
- 2 pinches sugar (optional)
- 2 Tbs parsley, chopped

Cauliflower steak:
- 1 tight head cauliflower
- 3 Tbs extra-virgin olive oil
- 3 Tbs butter
- Salt and pepper to taste

You might not believe that a head of cauliflower can make a quick meal for two or three people, but surprisingly, it can.

Clean away the greenery from a head of cauliflower, but leave the core intact. Trim the stem so that it's flat on the bottom. To make the steaks, cut about an inch off each side of the cauliflower. Those pieces will fall away because there isn't any core to hold them together. Reserve the excess pieces for another use, such as in a frittata. Cut the remaining cauliflower in half, then in half again to get four steaks.

Heat a pan on the stovetop and add some oil. Put in the steaks and season with salt and pepper. You should hear them sizzle as they cook. If you see smoke coming out of the pan, turn the heat down. If you don't hear any noise at all, turn the heat up. The challenges with this step are to brown the outside of the cauliflower and make sure it cooks all the way through, which will probably take about 4 or 5 minutes per side. If you notice that the cauliflower isn't browning evenly, you might add a bit more oil. Toward the end of the sauté time, add some butter to the pan; you want to get the flavor of the butter, but you don't want to take the risk that it will burn by adding it too early. To test for doneness, slide a knife in and make sure it goes in and comes out easily. If the cauliflower is getting too brown but is not yet done, you can slide the pan into a 350° oven to finish the dish.

The pan sauce for the cauliflower steaks uses pancetta or bacon, golden raisins, capers, parsley, and lemon juice. This kind of savory-sweet-tart sauce is often served on fish, but it's appropriate for these steaks, as well. Cook the bacon in a pan and then add the raisins and capers.

Add water and a splash of lemon juice to deglaze the pan, scraping the browned bacon or pancetta off the bottom. You want to achieve a nice balance among the sweetness of the raisins, the saltiness of the bacon and capers, and the tartness of the lemon juice. You actually want the sauce to be a little too tart at this point because you will swirl in some butter to calm it down.

The next step is to **mount** the sauce with butter. Mounting is a French technique that involves stirring butter into a sauce toward the end of the cooking process.

Keep stirring and make sure that the sauce doesn't boil too hard. The goal is for the butter to emulsify into the sauce without breaking into fat and butter solids. The closer the sauce gets to dry—that is, the more water that leaves the sauce—the more unstable the emulsion becomes. With water present, the butter doesn't break, but as the water boils away, the sauce becomes less and less stable, so don't boil it for too long.

To serve, top the cauliflower steaks with sauce and a sprinkle of parsley.

Grilled Endive with Tomato Carpaccio and Pulled Parsley Salad

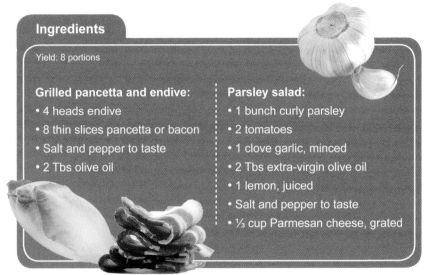

Ingredients

Yield: 8 portions

Grilled pancetta and endive:
- 4 heads endive
- 8 thin slices pancetta or bacon
- Salt and pepper to taste
- 2 Tbs olive oil

Parsley salad:
- 1 bunch curly parsley
- 2 tomatoes
- 1 clove garlic, minced
- 2 Tbs extra-virgin olive oil
- 1 lemon, juiced
- Salt and pepper to taste
- ⅓ cup Parmesan cheese, grated

When you're hungry for a small meal, a hot salad sometimes seems more substantial and satisfying than a cold one. To make this salad, cut a head of endive in half, wrap a slice of bacon around each half, and put these "packages" on a griddle or grill for about 5 minutes per side. The endive should be cooked through, and the bacon should be crisp.

In the meantime, make the dressing, using some of the vinaigrette we made earlier as a base. Because this salad contains parsley, which is an assertive green, the dressing also needs to be assertive. Give the vinaigrette a good shake, pour out a small portion in a bowl, and add some extra lemon juice, salt, and pepper. Add some garlic, too, which will give the dressing the strength and personality it needs to stand up to the parsley. Add the parsley to the bowl and toss; it can sit for about 30 minutes and will only get better. Taste the parsley and decide if it needs a bit more of any of the elements you just added. You

might also add some Parmesan cheese. You want the vinaigrette to be too flavorful, too tart, and too cheesy. Once you taste it with the parsley, you'll see that it's just right.

Next, slice two different colors of tomatoes into very thin slices (**carpaccio**). Arrange the tomatoes on a plate, season, and drizzle with dressing. Top with the endive packages and spoon the parsley salad around the edges of the plate. Grate some cheese on top and serve with a glass of wine.

Important Terms

carpaccio: Usually refers to a dish made with thinly sliced raw beef; also applies to other thinly sliced ingredients, such as tomatoes.

pappa al pomodoro: An Italian soup made with tomatoes and croutons.

mount: Refers to a French cooking technique that involves stirring butter into a sauce toward the end of the cooking process.

umami: A savory taste that demands a good deal of seasoning.

A Chef Entertains

Lesson 6

L ike you, chefs cook for themselves every day, but what they really enjoy is cooking for others. One way for anyone to relieve the drudgery of cooking daily meals is to throw a party for friends. When a chef entertains, he or she breaks down the work into manageable tasks and leverages what's on hand in the refrigerator, freezer, and pantry. Chefs also plan ahead, prepping and storing foods in the days leading up to the party. In this lesson, we'll make some hors d'oeuvres, a salad, and two entrées—all of which can be put together easily yet will still impress your guests.

Sautéed Green Beans with Pepper Flakes, Rosemary, and Lemon Zest

Ingredients

Yield: 6 portions

- 1 lb green beans
- Salt to taste
- ¼ cup olive oil
- 4 cloves garlic, minced
- ¼–½ tsp pepper flakes

- 1 ½ Tbs rosemary, chopped fine
- Zest of 1 lemon
- 1 Tbs unsalted butter

Start your party off with a little show by sautéing green beans as guests gather in the kitchen. The day before the party, begin by blanching the green beans. Note that as soon as you start cooking any green vegetable, the color degrades. The challenge here is to cook the beans quickly in boiling, salted water and cool them down immediately by plunging them in ice water. After the beans have cooled, drain them and store in a plastic bag with a paper towel inside to absorb any excess moisture.

The beans will serve as finger food at the party. When your guests arrive, heat a pan and add some olive oil. Put the beans in first, before the garlic, to make sure the garlic doesn't burn and become bitter. Next, add rosemary and pepper flakes. Toss the beans until they are heated through but not limp. Sprinkle on salt and lemon zest. Don't use lemon juice because its acidity will cause the beans to lose their color. At the very end of cooking, add a bit of butter. Transfer the beans to a platter and serve as an hors d'oeuvre.

Arancini

When chefs look in the refrigerator, they don't see leftovers; they see possibilities. You can make another quick hors d'oeuvre for the party from the leftover osso buco and risotto we made earlier. Form the rice into small, round croquettes by shaping it with your hands. (Wet your hands to keep the rice from sticking.) Make a hollow in the rice with your thumb, into which you can insert some of the braised meat, a piece of cheese, or both. Cover the filling with the rice to create what the Italians call **arancini** ("little oranges").

The next step is to bread the arancini by dipping them into egg and then bread crumbs. When you're breading any food, try to use one hand for dry ingredients and one for wet ingredients. Use your "wet hand" to dip the food into the egg and your "dry hand" to cover it with bread crumbs. This method prevents you from breading your own hands.

Arancini can be fried ahead of time and reheated briefly (for about 15 minutes) in a 300° oven. The idea is to warm the meat inside and soften the cheese but make sure the outside stays crusty. Drain the fried arancini on a pan covered with a paper towel and pop the pan into the oven just before you're ready to serve.

A variation on arancini is **supplì al telefono**. These are oblong shapes stuffed with cheese. When you're eating them, a "telephone wire" of cheese connects your mouth to your hand, giving these treats their name.

Dates with Cheese, Arugula, and Cracked Pepper

Ingredients

Yield: 8 portions

- 8 dates
- 8 shaved slices sharp Manchego or Pecorino cheese
- ¾ cup baby arugula

- 1 Tbs extra-virgin olive oil
- Sea salt and freshly ground black pepper to taste

Another hors d'oeuvre that can be made ahead of time is dates with Manchego or Pecorino cheese. Simply slice open some dates and tuck a piece of the cheese inside. Just before the party, cover a platter with arugula leaves, arrange the dates on top, drizzle with olive oil, and season with salt and freshly ground pepper. Encourage your guests to take a date with a leaf or two of arugula.

Grilled Prawns Wrapped in Pancetta with Lime and Cilantro

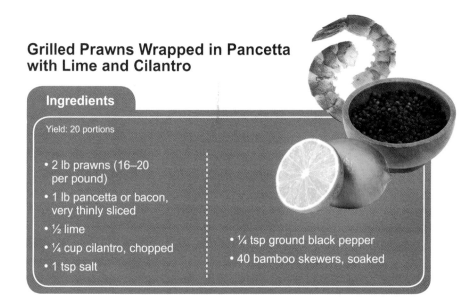

Ingredients

Yield: 20 portions

- 2 lb prawns (16–20 per pound)
- 1 lb pancetta or bacon, very thinly sliced
- ½ lime
- ¼ cup cilantro, chopped
- 1 tsp salt
- ¼ tsp ground black pepper
- 40 bamboo skewers, soaked

For one more do-ahead hors d'oeuvre, wrap some prawns with bacon. Insert two skewers in each to make turning on the grill easier. When the party starts, assign one of your guests to grill the prawns. When they're done, squeeze half a lime over the top and sprinkle on chopped parsley or cilantro.

Panzanella with Fresh Tomatoes, Cheese, and Herbs

Ingredients

Yield: 6-8 portions

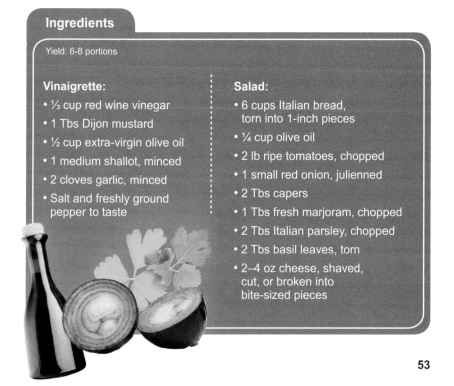

Vinaigrette:
- ⅓ cup red wine vinegar
- 1 Tbs Dijon mustard
- ½ cup extra-virgin olive oil
- 1 medium shallot, minced
- 2 cloves garlic, minced
- Salt and freshly ground pepper to taste

Salad:
- 6 cups Italian bread, torn into 1-inch pieces
- ¼ cup olive oil
- 2 lb ripe tomatoes, chopped
- 1 small red onion, julienned
- 2 Tbs capers
- 1 Tbs fresh marjoram, chopped
- 2 Tbs Italian parsley, chopped
- 2 Tbs basil leaves, torn
- 2–4 oz cheese, shaved, cut, or broken into bite-sized pieces

This bread salad will accompany both of the entrées to be served at the party. Begin by **macerating** the tomatoes overnight with some red onion, capers, coarsely chopped parsley, olive oil, vinegar, and salt. You can also toss in a few leaves of basil or some oregano or dill. To this mixture, add some shavings of Manchego or Parmesan, crumbled goat or feta cheese, or knobs of Brie. The delicious juices that form overnight will be absorbed by the same croutons we made for tomato soup earlier in the week. If you still have leftover vinaigrette, you can use that in place of additional olive oil and vinegar.

As the guests are enjoying hors d'oeuvres, transfer the tomatoes and cheese to a bowl, along with the accumulated juices. Taste and add more dressing if necessary. Toss together with the croutons and a few handfuls of arugula. Set aside at room temperature to serve with the entrées.

Chimichurri Sauce

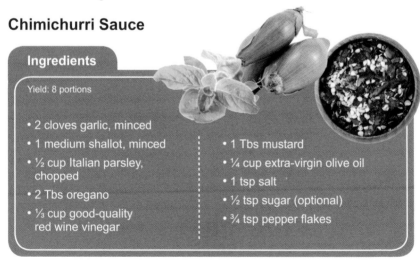

Ingredients

Yield: 8 portions

- 2 cloves garlic, minced
- 1 medium shallot, minced
- ½ cup Italian parsley, chopped
- 2 Tbs oregano
- ⅓ cup good-quality red wine vinegar

- 1 Tbs mustard
- ¼ cup extra-virgin olive oil
- 1 tsp salt
- ½ tsp sugar (optional)
- ¾ tsp pepper flakes

A simple **chimichurri** sauce goes well with grilled steak. Think of chimichurri as a sharp, herbal vinaigrette. Start by mixing shallots, garlic, pepper flakes, and salt with mustard and vinegar. To this, add olive oil, parsley, and oregano. The chimichurri should be a fairly thick sauce and assertive.

Grilled Steak

A good strategy to use, whether you're planning to serve fish or meat at a party, is to cook one large piece that can serve multiple people, rather than cooking individual portions. A porterhouse steak cut extra thick (about 2.5 inches) is a good choice. On one side of the T-bone is a piece of filet; on the other side is a New York strip.

Season and oil the porterhouse and put it on the grill before your guests arrive. As it cooks, pay attention to the way it sounds. Listen for a satisfying sizzle. After you've put grill marks on both sides, transfer the steak to a 300° oven. This lower temperature gives the heat the opportunity to penetrate the meat. For medium rare, take the steak out of the oven when a thermometer inserted into the thickest part (and not touching the bone) registers 128°. Set the steak aside to rest for 10 or 15 minutes to allow the pressure that has built up inside it while it was in the oven to subside and the juices to flow back into the meat.

Instead of making a sauce on the side, create a **board dressing** for this steak. This is nothing more than the chimichurri sauce we made earlier mixed with the juices on the cutting board after you've carved the meat. Spoon some of the sauce on the meat and even onto the board, allowing it to mingle with the meat juices. When guests serve themselves, encourage them to dip up some of the juices and sauce along with the meat. Sprinkle the steak with parsley and serve.

Sweet and Spicy Plank-Roasted Salmon

Ingredients

Yield: 8 portions

- 1 cup brown sugar
- ¼ cup soy sauce
- 1 tsp cayenne

- Zest of 1 orange
- 1–2 Tbs lemon juice
- 1 side of salmon, skin on and boned

To make a plank-roasted side of salmon, you first need a cedar plank. You can pick this up from the hardware store or lumberyard, but make sure you get untreated cedar, not flooring. Soak the plank in water so that it doesn't catch fire.

Ask your fish supplier for a side of salmon with the pin bones and scales removed. You can remove the small piece of backbone that remains yourself. When you get a large piece of fish, run your hands over it to feel where the bones are; after it's been cleaned and boned, it should feel smooth. If the fish is too large for your plank, trim off a small amount of the tail or belly meat. Center the salmon on the plank and score it into a diamond pattern. The purpose of this step is to create more surface area to enable the flavoring to get into the fish.

In a bowl, mix soy sauce, lemon juice, orange zest, cayenne pepper, and brown sugar. Taste this mixture, looking for a good balance of all the elements: sweet, salty, savory, spicy, and acidic. Spoon the flavoring over the salmon and use it to baste the fish as it cooks. The sauce has enough sugar in it that it will brown nicely in a 400° oven. Place the plank on a pan to catch any sugar that drips off before you put the salmon in the oven. The

Balancing Meals

When you're having a party—or anytime—keep in mind that you don't have to serve a starch, vegetables, and a protein all on one plate. The starch can be part of the first course; the protein can be part of the entrée; and so on.

cooking time will be 8 to 10 minutes per inch of thickness, or about 20 minutes or so for a large piece. If you use a thermometer, take the fish out of the oven at 140° and allow it to rest until it reaches 145°. Even better, break open the salmon at its thickest part and make sure that it's cooked and translucent all the way through. Serve the salmon right from the board.

Dessert

For dessert, make life easy on yourself by buying some nice cookies and vanilla ice cream. Top the ice cream with a sweet, thick sherry.

Over the course of these lessons, you've learned how to work smarter in the kitchen and turn out delicious meals for your family day after day. At your party, relax, enjoy the fruits of your efforts, and accept the accolades of your friends!

Important Terms

arancini: Italian for "little oranges," these are fried balls of rice stuffed with meat or cheese and served as an appetizer.

board dressing: A sauce made with herbs mingled with the juices from sliced meat on the cutting board.

chimichurri: A sharp, herbal vinaigrette generally used as a sauce for grilled meats.

macerate: To steep in liquid in order to soften. For example, croutons may be macerated in tomato juice and vinaigrette to be used in a bread salad.

supplì al telefono: A variation of arancini made in an oblong shape and stuffed with cheese; its name comes from the fact that the cheese forms a "telephone wire" between the eater's mouth and hand.

Weekly Menu Planning

A week represents 21 meals and some number of between-meal snacks. From this list, let's remove 3 meals: a breakfast on the weekend (to be replaced by a glorious brunch), an evening meal out with someone special, and a luncheon that is either a business meeting or a chance to catch up with friends or family. Remaining are only 18 meals: 6 breakfasts, 6 lunches, and 6 dinners.

Use a template to develop a menu plan (see following pages), giving thought to generating "planned overs" and doing prep work for lunches or follow-on meals.

As you plan your menu for the week, ask yourself these questions:

- What do you want to eat?

- What ingredients do you have on hand in your freezer, refrigerator, or pantry?

- What ingredients are in season—in other words, are readily available, inexpensive, and of good quality?

- What ingredients speak to you—are so delicious that they will shape your menu in the week ahead?

- What is your current skill set? What are you capable of in the kitchen?

As your menu comes together, look for opportunities to repurpose "planned overs." These are not leftovers but foods that keep well and can be prepared in greater-than-needed quantities so that they can be used later to cobble together a quick meal. But avoid making more than you need of dishes that don't keep well or that quickly become monotonous.

Once you know what to cook, the next step is to make a shopping list, organized by broad themes: produce, meat and fish, dairy, frozen foods, dry goods, and household supplies. Taking the time to organize your shopping trip is much more efficient and less stressful that just winging it at the store. Even for a chef, shopping without a plan often results in the frustration of forgotten ingredients and additional trips to the store. Set aside some time in your week to tackle this important task.

And don't make shopping all work. Allow yourself to buy a couple of treats or items that hold special appeal: freshly baked bread, ripe fruit, a vegetable you love, such as sweet corn on the cob or ripe avocados. But don't get completely sidetracked and forget your weekly menu. Filling your house with food is not the goal; laying in the foods you need to realize your plan is.

Sample Menu Plan

Day of the Week	Breakfast	Lunch	Dinner	Prep/Planned-Overs
Monday	Breakfast at work	Chicken salad sandwich on flax bread, apples	Penne with Swiss chard	Cook double batch penne; use for Monday dinner and Wednesday lunch. Clean chard, rabe, romaine for Monday, Tuesday, and Wednesday dinners. Soak white beans and chickpeas for Wednesday and Thursday lunches. Hard boil eggs for Wednesday dinner.
Tuesday	Soy power shake with oat bran and flax	Lunch with co-workers	Rabe and bocconcini on toast	Simmer white beans in vegetable stock for Wednesday lunch . Simmer chickpeas in vegetable stock for Thursday lunch. Prepare large batch of vinaigrette for Thursday lunch and Wednesday and Thursday dinners. Soak dried fruits for Wednesday breakfast.
Wednesday	Oatmeal with plumped dried fruits	Bean and pasta soup	Niçoise salad	Steam and chill crab, shrimp, and scallops for Thursday and Friday dinners. Cut fruit for Thursday breakfast. Prep Greek salad for Thursday lunch.
Thursday	Fruit salad	Greek salad with chickpeas	Cold crab, apple, and endive salad	Prep vegetables for ceviche for Friday dinner. Cut tortillas and bake half for Friday dinner; save remainder for Sunday brunch.
Friday	Blueberry smoothie	Department head lunch meeting	Ceviche with baked corn chips	Steam couscous for Saturday dinner. Make tomato salsa for Friday dinner and Sunday brunch. Brine Cornish hens for Saturday dinner.
Saturday	Fruit and yogurt with granola	Heirloom tomato toast	BBQ Cornish hens, couscous, and fresh herb salad	Cook one extra hen for Monday lunch next week.
Sunday	Chilaquiles (brunch)		Dinner out	None

Menu-Planning Template

Day of the Week	Breakfast	Lunch	Dinner	Prep/Planned-Overs
Monday				
Tuesday				
Wednesday				
Thursday				
Friday				
Saturday				
Sunday				

To download and print this template, go to www.thegreatcourses.com, log in to your customer account, select "Course Starter Materials," and then select *The Everyday Gourmet: Making Great Meals in Less Time.*

Glossary

aioli: Mayonnaise flavored with garlic.

airline chicken breast: A boneless chicken breast with part of the wing still attached.

arancini: Italian for "little oranges," these are fried balls of rice stuffed with meat or cheese and served as an appetizer.

board dressing: A sauce made with herbs mingled with the juices from sliced meat on the cutting board.

bouquet garni: A small package of herbs tied together and cooked with a dish but removed before serving.

carpaccio: Usually refers to a dish made with thinly sliced raw beef; also applies to other thinly sliced ingredients, such as tomatoes.

chiffonade: Finely sliced or shredded herbs or vegetables; often used as a garnish.

chimichurri: A sharp, herbal vinaigrette generally used as a sauce for grilled meats.

chorizo: Spicy Spanish sausage.

condimenti: Refers to finishing ingredients of a dish, such as butter, grated cheese, and so on.

emulsifier: In cooking, an ingredient that helps hold otherwise immiscible liquids, such as oil and water, together in a mixture.

farro: An ancient form of wheat.

frittata: A dish that's similar to an omelet but unfolded. A good vehicle for using up leftover vegetables and preparing a quick meal.

gremolata: A condiment made from chopped parsley, garlic, and lemon zest.

macerate: To steep in liquid in order to soften. For example, croutons may be macerated in tomato juice and vinaigrette to be used in a bread salad.

mount: Refers to a French cooking technique that involves stirring butter into a sauce toward the end of the cooking process.

pappa al pomodoro: An Italian soup made with tomatoes and croutons.

pekmez: Grape molasses used in Turkey.

roux: A combination of flour and fat, cooked together and used to thicken soups or sauces.

sofrito: Flavor base.

spelt: An ancient form of wheat.

supplì al telefono: A variation of arancini made in an oblong shape and stuffed with cheese; its name comes from the fact that the cheese forms a "telephone wire" between the eater's mouth and hand.

tahini: Sesame paste; used to make hummus or baba ghanoush.

truss: To wrap meat with string to hold it together while it cooks.

umami: A savory taste that demands a good deal of seasoning.

Bibliography

Note: All books listed below are available on the website of The Culinary Institute of America at http://www.ciaprochef.com/fbi/.

Conniff-Dobrich, Cate. *Seasons in the Wine Country: Recipes from The Culinary Institute of America at Greystone.* San Francisco: Chronicle Books, 2010.

The Culinary Institute of America (CIA). *Breakfasts and Brunches.* New York: Lebhar-Friedman, 2005.

———. *Cooking at Home with The Culinary Institute of America.* New York: Wiley, 2003.

———. *The Culinary Institute of America Cookbook: A Collection of Our Favorite Recipes for the Home Chef.* New York: Lebhar-Friedman, 2008.

———. *Gourmet Meals in Minutes.* New York: Lebhar-Friedman, 2004.

———. *Grilling: Exciting International Flavors from the World's Premier Culinary College.* New York: Lebhar-Friedman, 2006.

———. *Healthy Cooking at Home with The Culinary Institute of America.* New York: Wiley, 2011.

———. *The New Book of Soups.* New York: Lebhar-Friedman, 2009.

———. *One Dish Meals.* New York: Lebhar-Friedman, 2006.

———. *Pasta: Classic and Contemporary Pasta, Risotto, Crespelle, and Polenta Recipes.* Hoboken, NJ: John Wiley & Sons, 2013.

———. *The Professional Chef.* 9th ed. New York: Wiley, 2001. (The online version of this book can be found at https://www.inkling.com/store/professional-chef-cia-9th/.)

———. *Vegetables.* New York: Lebhar-Friedman, 2007.

———, Mark Erickson, and Lisa Erickson. *Cooking for One: A Seasonal Guide to the Pleasure of Preparing Delicious Meals for Yourself.* New York: Lebhar-Friedman, 2011.

———— and Ben Fink. *Hors d'Oeuvre at Home with The Culinary Institute of America*. New York: Wiley, 2007.

———— and Lynne Gigliotti. *Mediterranean Cooking*. Boston: Houghton Mifflin Harcourt, 2013.

———— and Abigail Kirsch. *Entertaining: Recipes and Inspirations for Gathering with Family and Friends*. Hoboken, NJ: John Wiley & Sons, 2012.

———— and Katherine Polenz. *Vegetarian Cooking at Home with The Culinary Institute of America*. New York: Wiley, 2012.

————, Gianni Scappin, Alberto Vanoli, and Steven Kolpan. *Italian Cooking at Home with The Culinary Institute of America*. New York: Wiley, 2011.

———— and Martha Rose Shulman. *Culinary Boot Camp: Five Days of Basic Training at The Culinary Institute of America*. New York: Wiley, 2006.

Fischer, John W., and Lou Jones. *Bistros and Brasseries: Recipes and Reflections on Classic Café Cooking*. New York: Lebhar-Friedman, 2008.

Scappin, Gianni, and Vincenzo Lauria. *A Tavola! Recipes and Reflections on Traditional Italian Home Cooking*. New York: Lebhar-Friedman, 2009.

Shulman, Martha Rose. *Spain and the World Table*. New York: DK Adult, 2011.

Recipe List

Photographic Credits

Page i: © iStockphoto/Thinkstock.

Page iv: © iStockphoto/Thinkstock.

Page 1:   © iStockphoto/Thinkstock.

Page 2:   © iStockphoto/Thinkstock.

Page 3:   © iStockphoto/Thinkstock.

Page 4:   © Hemera/Thinkstock.

Page 5:   © iStockphoto/Thinkstock.

Page 6:   Justin Smith @JustinTimePhoto.com.

Page 7:   © PhotoObjects.net/Thinkstock.

Page 8:   © iStockphoto/Thinkstock.

Page 9:   ©Brand X Pictures/Thinkstock. © iStockphoto/Thinkstock.

Page 10:   Justin Smith @JustinTimePhoto.com.

Page 13:   © iStockphoto/Thinkstock.

Page 14:   Justin Smith @JustinTimePhoto.com.

Page 15:   © iStockphoto/Thinkstock.

Page 16:   © iStockphoto/Thinkstock.

Page 17:   Justin Smith @JustinTimePhoto.com.

Page 18:   © iStockphoto/Thinkstock.

Page 20:   © iStockphoto/Thinkstock.

Page 21:   Justin Smith @JustinTimePhoto.com.

Page 22:   © iStockphoto/Thinkstock.

Page 23:   ©Creatas Images/Creatas/Thinkstock. © iStockphoto/Thinkstock.
            © Wavebreak Media/Thinkstock

Page 24:   © iStockphoto/Thinkstock.

Page 25:   Justin Smith @JustinTimePhoto.com.

Page 26:   © iStockphoto/Thinkstock.

Page 27:   © iStockphoto/Thinkstock. Justin Smith @JustinTimePhoto.com.

Page 28:   © iStockphoto/Thinkstock.

Page 29:   Justin Smith @JustinTimePhoto.com.

Page 31:   Justin Smith @JustinTimePhoto.com.

Page 32:   Justin Smith @JustinTimePhoto.com.

Page 33:   © iStockphoto/Thinkstock.

Page 34:   © iStockphoto/Thinkstock.

Page 35:   Justin Smith @JustinTimePhoto.com.

Page 36:   © iStockphoto/Thinkstock. © George Doyle/Stockbyte/Thinkstock.

Page 37: Justin Smith @JustinTimePhoto.com.

Page 38: Justin Smith @JustinTimePhoto.com.

Page 39: © iStockphoto/Thinkstock.

Page 40: Justin Smith @JustinTimePhoto.com.

Page 41: © iStockphoto/Thinkstock.

Page 42: © iStockphoto/Thinkstock. Justin Smith @JustinTimePhoto.com.

Page 43: Justin Smith @JustinTimePhoto.com.

Page 44: © iStockphoto/Thinkstock.

Page 45: © iStockphoto/Thinkstock. Justin Smith @JustinTimePhoto.com.

Page 46: © iStockphoto/Thinkstock.

Page 47: Justin Smith @JustinTimePhoto.com.

Page 48: Justin Smith @JustinTimePhoto.com.

Page 49: © iStockphoto/Thinkstock.

Page 50: Justin Smith @JustinTimePhoto.com.

Page 51: © iStockphoto/Thinkstock. Justin Smith @JustinTimePhoto.com.

Page 52: Justin Smith @JustinTimePhoto.com.

Page 53: © iStockphoto/Thinkstock.

Page 54: © iStockphoto/Thinkstock. Justin Smith @JustinTimePhoto.com.

Page 55: Justin Smith @JustinTimePhoto.com.

Page 56: Justin Smith @JustinTimePhoto.com.

Page 57: © Hemera/Thinkstock. © iStockphoto/Thinkstock.

Page 58: Justin Smith @JustinTimePhoto.com.

Page 59: © iStockphoto/Thinkstock.

Page 60: © iStockphoto/Thinkstock.

Page 64: © iStockphoto/Thinkstock.

Page 66: © iStockphoto/Thinkstock.

Page 67: © iStockphoto/Thinkstock.

Notes: © iStockphoto/Thinkstock.

Notes

Notes

Notes